Sermons from New Hope

Kerri Mock Hefner

Parson's Porch Books
www.parsonsporchbooks.com

Sermons from New Hope
ISBN: Softcover 978-1-951472-22-1
Copyright © 2019 by Kerri Mock Hefner

All rights reserved. No part of this book may be reproduced or transmitted in any form or by any means, electronic or mechanical, including photocopying, recording, or by any information storage and retrieval system, without permission in writing from the publisher.

Sermons from New Hope

Contents

Introduction 7

Part I: Do Not Be Afraid

The Word of the Lord Was Rare 11
   1 Samuel 3:1-20; Ephesians 4:1-6

His Grace Has Not Been in Vain 18
   2 Corinthians 15:1-11

Do Not Be Afraid 23
   Isaiah 7:10-16; Matthew 1:18-25

We Are Not Afraid 28
   1 John 4: 7-21

Ministering to the Fearful 34
   1 Kings 19:9-18; Matthew 14:22-33

Christ Is Present in Unlikely Places 39
   Luke 2:1-20

Part II: Bloom Where You're Planted

Mental Health Month 45
   Acts 11:1-18; Revelation 21:1-6

Mary and Martha 51
   Luke 10:38-42

The Prodigal Son 55
   Luke 15:11-32

Honoring One Another 60
   1 Samuel 1:4-20, Mark 13:1-8

Falling in Love 65
    Luke 5:1-11
Bloom Where You're Planted 68
    Jeremiah 29:1, 4-7; Luke 17:11-19
Home by Another Way 71
    Matthew 2:1-12

Part III: You've Got This

Hope in a Clay Jar 76
    2 Corinthians 4:5-12
Life Finds a Way 81
    John 20:1-18
Hope Does Not Disappoint 84
    Romans 5:1-5
The Call, the Cry, the Answer 87
    Isaiah 58:1-12
A Life of Love 92
    1 Corinthians 13
Pumpkin Spice 97
    John 18:33-37
They Remembered His Words 102
    John 20:1-18

Introduction

I was surprised and honored to receive an invitation to publish a collection of sermons. In assembling this collection of sermons, I realized a lot of my sermons have the same basic theme. Don't be afraid – bloom where you're planted – you've got this. I want to encourage listeners, not simply so they will feel better, but so they will find their way to active participation in God's good works.

Many of my preaching mentors encouraged me to "keep it simple." Bill Neely and Wanda Neely encouraged me to preach without notes, a method which makes the preacher keep to just a few key points. Kermit Dancy told me all sermon topics could be counted on one hand: God, Jesus Christ, the Holy Spirit, sin/forgiveness, and the church. David Bartlett challenged everyone in his preaching class to make sure there is Good News in each sermon. Steve Hayner asked me to look for what Christ is doing in the world, and to follow with words and actions.

So many women mentors have encouraged me and bolstered my resolve during almost twenty years of ordained ministry. I am thankful beyond words for Cherrie Henry, Carter Shelley, Susan Fricks, Carol Gregg, Susan Dunlap, and Wanda Neely, among many others.

In these times in which many of us feel stretched thin and stressed out, I hope the message of these sermons will provide encouragement to keep on going. Don't be afraid – bloom where you're planted – you've got this. God has called us to good work. May we respond to that call in faith, love, and hope.

With joy,
Kerri

Part I

Don't Be Afraid

The Word of the Lord Was Rare
1 Samuel 3:1-20; Ephesians 4:1-6

Ordination Sermon

(preached for a friend's ordination, in a small town that had lost a good portion of its economic base)

November 2018

Long ago, in a land far, far away, it was a gloomy and lonely time.

"The word of the Lord was rare in those times," we read in 1 Samuel.

As the story of Samuel begins, it stands in the shadow of the ending of the previous book, the book of Judges. "In those days," we read in Judges, "there was no king in Israel; all the people did what was right in their own eyes." (Judges 21:25)

To the Biblical writers the position of having each person decide what is right for himself or herself is not a good place to be.

Leadership is rare in this disorganized time. The word of the Lord is rare. Every person does what is right in his or her own eyes. Those who have the strength and capability for leadership use their position for their own gain.

There is much evil in this situation: the priests in particular, men in their prime, are scamming the people and filling their own bellies. It is like the "wild west," or like a post-apocalyptic movie such as *Mad Max* or *Waterworld*.

In this difficult situation, who is going to hear the Word of the Lord?

— the average man? Probably not. He's too busy figuring out his own life from day to day, as it says in Judges.

— the average woman? It doesn't look that way. She's like the average man, just trying to keep it together.

— the priest? No, too busy filling his own dish with choice leg of lamb.

This is a time when the Word is desperately needed but everyone is disconnected, and disaffected. In such an environment how is the Word going to break through? The word of the Lord would be a shot in the dark in this situation.

So, in this situation is an old priest, Eli. Helping Eli and serving in God's house is a youngster, Samuel.

The elderly Eli knew his sons, the priests, were in trouble. His sons were the priests filling their own bellies at the people's expense. God had already spoken to Eli about that.

Eli's darkness is growing ... his eyes don't work anymore, so his world is dark. He endures a long night of the soul, knowing his sons were doing evil and knowing God was displeased.

The Word of the Lord would be a shot in the dark in this situation. So God waits until dark ... until one dark night.

The boy Samuel needs some help figuring out what is happening. He knows about God, but he does not know God in a personal way. He's still a youngster, a doorkeeper and a helper.

Samuel's job was to open the door of the tabernacle. His job after that fateful night is to open the door and deliver the word of the Lord to his teacher.

It takes a while for him to understand. God helps him out ... speaking to the boy and also showing the divine presence to him.

Here's something the boy did not know.... The elderly leader whose eyesight was failing saw, or perceived that God was up to something. Eli was waiting for it. He knew Samuel would have a special role, when Samuel was just a teardrop falling from his mother's eye. You see, Eli had encountered Samuel's mother Hannah back when she was a lonely and sad woman, ashamed because she did not have a child in a world that devalued women without children. Eli wasn't sure about Hannah at first, but then he was able to see that her prayers and her tears were connected to God's plan.

As I mentioned a few moments ago, Eli also knew his sons were in deep trouble.

Yet God has a plan, even in this depressing time. God knows God's plan and waits. Eli knows God is up to something and waits.

The Word is not necessarily comforting to old Eli. Samuel hates to have to bring it to him.

Yet ... everything is laid out for Samuel to go and do as he is called... doors have already been opened for the young doorkeeper.

I wonder if the whole business of getting up and going to Eli three times in the middle of the night was part of God's plan... if somehow it was part of God opening the door for young Samuel. Samuel, as young as he was, could perhaps dismiss an odd feeling that comes and goes in the middle of the night. By speaking three times, God shows Samuel that this is real, and this is important.

I wonder if there's some closure and maybe even hope for old Eli. He knows he cannot change the past. Yet he also now knows .... God has a vision for the future. God has provided Israel with hope. As the text says, during this night of revelation, the lamp had not yet gone out. There is still hope.

So who perceives the word of the Lord in the first few chapters of Samuel? A sad woman ... a boy ... an old man who is blind and disappointed. Unlikely people. Yet they receive new hope.

In our New Testament reading, Ephesians 4:1-6, we read about hope.

Where is the hope today? Where is the Word of the Lord?

Who today does not know God? I'm not necessarily talking about people with no faith whatsoever. I'm thinking more about people who know God is out there somewhere but haven't had any reason to put their own faith in this seemingly distant God.

Where is the Word of the Lord today?
— People distrust institutions, corporations, evening news … things we trusted 50 years ago. The Word may not be showing up in the places where we are looking.
— Jobs are gone, and the types of work available now have changed.
— Yet people still want to hear something good… people hunger to hear good news.

The Word does show up… in unlikely places… amongst people barely even ready to hear it.

Your new pastor is someone who can help you hear God's word.

Your new pastor was a chaplain resident at a major teaching hospital for a year. In the hospital people are busy. There was one wife of a patient who took up an inordinate amount of the staff's time. The wife of the patient was labeled as "difficult." She made unrealistic demands. The staff did not want to see her, much less talk to her. So your new pastor invited the woman to reflect on her situation. She invited the woman to give herself a name, and the woman chose "The Lioness." Your new pastor informed the staff of the new name. She made no excuses for the woman's behavior, but just by naming the intense personality and the intense emotions, the staff was able to hear the woman anew. It was as if a door had been opened, allowing people to see and hear and perceive this woman's pain.

What you have here is a person who can open the door for you. Did you hear in the passage from 1 Samuel how little Samuel opened the door of the temple in the morning? That was his job, to open the door to God's house. Your new pastor will help you open the door. She will not sugarcoat the word of the Lord for you. She will help you to hear it. She will help you to act on it.

She will help you to find hope ... hope that begins in unlikely places ... like the hope that began with a young man and an elderly man who had lost his sight ... like the hope that began in the tabernacle that people didn't trust anymore.

It's all right if it takes you a while to hear or understand. Your pastor said it took her a while to hear the call in her own life.

She will help you live a life worthy of the calling to which you have been called.

Doors have been opened already. Young Samuel may have thought he was receiving a vision of something completely new ... yet God had already shown Eli some vision for the future.

God has already been in front you of laying a foundation of hope... opening doors that you didn't even realize you needed to go through. Crossing through some of those doorways can be frightening.

Today, allow God to be at work, opening the door of hope for you.

Lead a life worthy of your calling ... you are one body, and there is one Spirit ... you have the one hope of your calling.

Thanks be to God for opening the door that leads to hope. Thanks be to God for your new pastor, and may God bless this calling. Amen.

His Grace Has Not Been in Vain
2 Corinthians 15:1-11

Sermon for Meeting of Presbytery of New Hope
October 2011

I found a booklet in the historical collection of this congregation, the congregation which I serve as associate pastor. In this little tome one can read about all the Presbyterian churches in this area, circa 1960. Things have changed since this booklet was written. Church membership has declined. We as a denomination are building far fewer churches. Some of the towns represented in this booklet, and towns you may represent, have lost population over the last 20 or 30 years. Some of these churches depicted in the booklet are now closed.

Looking at this booklet made me feel sad. It feels like a bad time to be a Christian, the wrong time. Maybe it even feels like Jesus stopped making himself known.

Do you feel like you lost your purpose? Does it feel like others don't believe in you, or, heaven forbid, that you don't believe in yourself?

Perhaps you have a purpose, but is it healthy? Is your purpose and heart's desire that of some of the Christians in Corinth -- to be right, to be noticed, to be admired? If so then you may not like Paul, the author of today's reading. Something about Paul was not as attractive or admirable as the new Christians had hoped. Some folks even wanted to get away from Paul

-- he preached the truth, but they didn't like the package.

It's a tough time to be a Christian. We preach the same things Paul preached, and we get a reaction from the world that ranges from harassment to ho-hum.

We preach that you should read Scripture regularly, even the parts that are difficult to understand, like the end of Psalm 139.

We preach that you should give -- not just at Christmas, but often, regularly, and that you should give a lot.

We preach that you should worship in a community, where you will intentionally put yourself in the same pew as people who are not famous or successful or perfect.

We preach that the last shall be first and no one likes to hear that.

We preach that it's not about you ... it's about Jesus.

There are other gospels one can preach today. Perhaps a gospel of health and wealth, a gospel of things that always work out perfectly, a gospel based on a cult of personality ... but those gospels are vanity, preached and taught and lived in vain.

So do you feel like you've lost your purpose? Do you feel like you've found a vain purpose?

Or do you feel a call, a nudge from the Spirit, to do something else? Recently I've been studying under Steve Hayner at Columbia Theological Seminary. Dr. Hayner talked about our call. He said: the purpose of the church is to participate in Christ's ministries in the world. I love the way he makes it clear: not our ministries, not even something that we have to be clever and create. It's *Christ's* ministries, things that are already happening because Christ started them. And when Jesus gets something started, his grace is not in vain.

The purpose of the church is to participate in Christ's ministries in the world. What are some those ministries?

   * people make long journeys on foot to hospitals founded by Presbyterians because they know they will get good care, even if they are outcast

   * students flock to schools founded and staffed by Presbyterians

   * children who have been abused and neglected find safety in Presbyterian homes across the US

And they all witness the work of Christ, Kingdom work, being done on their behalf. As much as they may struggle day to day, they learn that God's grace is not in vain -- it is real, and alive, and blossoming in their lives.

Remember that booklet featuring some now-defunct churches? Here in town, I can think of three congregations that were founded since that booklet was produced. It ain't over yet!

The church I served in my first call, a 150- member church in a small town that has lost much of its economic base, is real and alive. That church started a program with the local department of social services, strengthening marriages and families through classes held in the church fellowship hall. People who wondered if a church would judge them for their difficult family circumstances felt welcomed, and grateful.

His grace is not in vain.

Who in your community may be wondering whether God's grace is in vain? Whether God cares? Could it be the people who have lost jobs? The people who have spent years getting a good education and now can't find work? Perhaps you live in an area where a significant portion of the population has never had economic opportunity. Perhaps you are living in an area where people are affluent but are finding that money can't buy the perfect life for which they had hoped.

We can draw a lot of inspiration from Paul. Here was a man of formidable intelligence (I'm exhausted every time I read Romans!) and yet he managed to tell regular people about the faith in such a way that they dropped everything and believed. We may not have the most modern buildings or the latest musical instruments, but we have a story to tell and grace to share.

Jesus is already ministering in our midst. His grace is not in vain.

Where in your community is Christ already ministering, and how can you get on board?

Do Not Be Afraid
Isaiah 7:10-16; Matthew 1:18-25

Sunday after a crisis in the congregation

The year was 735 BC. King Ahaz of Judah felt pressure from neighboring Israel and Syria. The specter of the Assyrian empire was on the horizon, and international relations had become complicated. Syria and Israel wanted help, and they laid pressure on him. Ahaz appealed to king of Assyria for help, promised to be his vassal, even gave him sacred objects from the temple as a pledge.

The prophet Isaiah came to tell him that the pressure would be off soon and pointed to a young woman. Which young woman we don't know, but he said that by the time the young woman's child had learned to tell good from bad, the crisis would be over.

It was too late for Ahaz. He had already made his decision to find the quickest way out.

Fast forward 700 plus years to an engaged couple facing serious pressure. You may be familiar with Mary's story in the book of Luke -- today we have the story of Joseph, Mary's fiancé. According to Luke, Mary was able to escape some pressure by staying with her cousin Elizabeth for a good portion of her pregnancy. We encounter Joseph today, trying to figure out how he will get some relief from the pressure of having a fiancée who is already expecting a baby.

To make sure Joseph heard the message, God sent an angel with the message, do not be afraid. Do not be afraid, God has this situation handled. And God has plans for you.

The situation for Joseph is frightening. It's embarrassing at the least, dangerous to reputations of individuals and families. At the worst, the situation could fatal for Mary, who could be punished by stoning. Joseph has decided to find a way out of this pressure, this situation of being between a rock and a hard place -- he plans to dismiss her quietly, whatever that means. Then the angel comes.

Do you hear the words of the angel? Do you hear the words of the prophet?

Do not be afraid. God will give you a sign. Immanuel, God-With-Us.

The world we live in seems like a place to be afraid. It seems like a world of grief -- a world where things always end. A world where at the worst, things crash down around us, and at the best we are stuck in impossible places with nothing but terrible choices ahead of us.

Today you may feel like you've arrived at one of those impossible places. A place where you have so many feelings boiling over you don't know what to do. A place where you feel like the floor has been pulled out from under you, and you're in a free fall. A place where you can't see any good coming out of it.

Right now, in this moment, maybe that's where you need to be. You may not want to be in this impossible situation. You may feel drawn to a quick solution just to ease the pain and pressure. Yet ... you know, patching things over can ease the pain for a while but won't work forever.

You may be here today burdened by pressures from many different kinds of situations. Maybe you feel that everything in your life is too much and you can't see a way clear to get some relief. Maybe you feel boxed into a corner, maybe you've made some choices that brought you to this corner. And maybe now you fear that you have a lot to lose, and you need to protect what little you have left. We fear losing everything, don't we? We fear falling apart, looking like fools, being exposed or humiliated. Some poor decisions can come from looking for quick relief.

Right now, in this moment, I can tell you that other people know that story. You are not alone.

I simply hope to tell you today that Scripture has a larger story. In the story of Scripture, God sees those impossible places, and sees the people stuck in those places. And God says, do not be afraid.

Do not be afraid. There are other places besides this corner, the place where the pressure feels too great.

We may be in a place where we feel beat down and burdened, worried and restless. But God promises to lift us up and help us. Hear these words from the

Gospel of Matthew: "Come all ye who are weak and heavy laden, and I will give you rest." (Matthew 11:28)

You might see a dead end, but God sees a new trail. It might have a lot of briars, but it's a trail that will lead you somewhere. Hear these words from the letter to the Philippians: "I can do all things through Christ who strengthens me." (Philippians 4:13)

We may be in a place where anger and anxiety put pressure on us, and make it hard to breathe, but God brings us to fresh air. Hear these words from the Psalmist: "He makes me lie down in green pastures, he leads be beside still waters, he restores my soul." (Psalm 23:2-3)

We may be in a place where all we can see is the way of death, but God knows the way of life. God sent this baby Jesus, God with us, Immanuel, to bring us into that way of life. Hear more from Matthew: "I will be with you always, even unto the end of the age." (Matthew 28:20)

Do not be afraid. Do not be afraid. Call his name Jesus and know that God is with us.

Christians, God is with us, and God gives us work to do. Prayer and fellowship. Watching and waiting. Caring for one another. Working out how we feel, and what we will do, without rushing to the quickest answer. We have the work of caring for those most vulnerable.

God gives us the strength and the grace to do the work.

In this difficult time I hope you will keep going. Come to church and to our activities. Read the daily Bible selection at pcusa.org — it's surprising how the selection will speak to you. Talk to me. Don't go it alone. And do not be afraid. Amen.

We Are Not Afraid
1 John 4: 7-21

Lent 2019

Many of you are familiar with the gospel song and protest anthem "We Shall Overcome." One of the verses in the song goes, "We are not afraid ..." This song came to mind as I read this passage for today, especially the part about how perfect love casts out fear. So the title of the sermon is We Are Not Afraid. Just to be clear, I'm going to talk about love for a while, but then I will get back to the idea of not being afraid.

We have been reading from this book, 1 John, for a few weeks in worship. First John is a letter, written to a community of Christians very early in the history of the church.

We have learned a lot from John these last few weeks. Last week our teenagers led our service and reminded us of the words from 1 John chapter 3, let us love in truth and action.

We also read from 1 John; God is light. We are children of God.

And today, we read more about love.

What is God's love like?

God loves like a child ... sincerely, earnestly.

God loves like no adult can ... eternally, unflinchingly.

Christians believe the person and work of Jesus Christ was God's bold expression of love for the world. Jesus' teaching, healing, death and resurrection — all for people like us, people who make mistakes, people who sin, people who don't love God back — it was all God's act of love.

And, Christians believe, this act of love gave life. Death is not the final answer, and sin is not our ultimate fate. In Jesus' death and resurrection, everything has been made subject to Jesus Christ, whom Christians call Lord and Savior.

Some Christians may read this passage about love and think it sounds mushy. They are looking for the God of judgment and maybe even the God of vengeance. If anyone is looking for that particular God, I recommend going back to the Hebrew prophets: Amos, Isaiah, Hosea. The prophets give God's judgment for disobedience and sin, but the prophets also give a hope for reconciliation. And reconciliation is part of ... love.

Perfect love casts out fear ... we are not afraid.

John's writing on love is one of those passages of Scripture that carry deep meaning in a few words. You could carry these few lines with you and read them often, and still not plumb the depths of what this means.

Let's take a moment for academic study. This passage has a chiastic structure, meaning that the author digs down to a central meaning, then repeats on his or her way back up. A chiastic structure is like eating a baked good filled with something delicious. Think about a pie with a top and bottom crust. My favorite pie is a fried pie, a pie shell folded over apple cinnamon filling, and of course fried. Anyway, with the two-crust pie, you begin by eating some tasty crust, then get to a little of the filling, then a good bite of that delicious filling, then you're back to the edge with more crust. So here's the apple fried pie of what John is saying.

The crust is, let us love one another. The passage begins and ends, with the exhortation to love one another. Even if you forget the filling, remember the crust: love one another.

Working in toward the middle, we read: love comes from God. God loves us, then we are able to love. Love is a sacrifice: it wipes out sin and fear.

We learn more about love: God lives in us, makes a home with us, when we love others.

And more: this relationship of love gives us knowledge of a unseen God. No one has ever seen God, but in our love for one another we make a space for God to become known.

And finally to the filling, which is a statement of faith. We have received God's Spirit. The Father has sent the Son as Savior.

And then we work our way back to the crust of the pie... God is known to us in love ... love helps us be bold and unafraid ... God abides in us ... let us love one another.

(Note to readers: I diagrammed the chiastic structure of the passage and with hand gestures indicated how the passage went toward the center and back out.)

```
Let us love one another
    Loving is of God
        God's love revealed to us through Son, not that we
        loved God, but that God loved us
            Love is the atoning sacrifice
                If we love one another, God lives in us, and
                    his love is perfected in us
                    No one has ever seen God, but if we
                    love we know we abide in him
                    He has given us of his Spirit.
                    We see & testify that the Father
                        has sent his Son as the Savior of
                        the world.

                If we confess our faith, God abides in us
                        and we in God, and we know and
                        believe
            God abides in us; love has been perfected
                in us
        Love helps us be bold, there is no fear in love
    We love because he first loved us
  Not loving is not of God
Commandment:  love one another
```

This is the type of Scripture that makes for solid spiritual food.

And yet so often, we choose not to allow God to nourish us with love.

Who nourishes or feeds your spirit? Are you being fed with solid spiritual food?

Do you have anyone in your life who eggs on your fears? Spiritually and emotionally some people are feeding themselves with fear. Online, a lonely or fearful or alienated person can find something to stoke those fears, nurture those feelings of alienation and rejection. The recruitment is all the same … whether for groups that promote an idea of racial or religious supremacy … those that promote violence … preach subjugation of women and minorities … whether it's ISIS or a white power group or any other website where violence is promoted … these websites stoke your fears and get you to do dirty work for the person sitting on the other side of the internet connection.

In fear and hatred, there is not a space for God to abide.

But who encourages your best? How will we encourage others to full of good things, not to be empty inside, not to be filled with rot?

Let us seek the good spiritual food, food that builds us up.

In conclusion, what is there to be afraid of? There are plenty of frightening things in the world, there is plenty of reason to be careful. Yet deep down, what's down here in the filling our hearts and spirits? Is it fear? Is it punishment? Hatred? Or is it God's love?

One of the most common phrases in the Bible is, do not be afraid. Jesus says it to his disciples. Angels say "do not be afraid" when they visit someone.

Let perfect love be the center of your life. Let perfect love feed you and take care of you. Let perfect love cast out fear. Thanks be to God for that perfect love.

Ministering to the Fearful
1 Kings 19:9-18; Matthew 14:22-33

Sunday after the white supremacist march in Charlottesville, VA

August 13, 2017

What makes a movie actor look like a bad guy? *The Wall Street Journal* featured an essay, "The Secret to Looking Sinister on Screen," on how the looks of the actor help the viewer distinguish the heroes from the villains. One way to accomplish the sinister look is to create or magnify facial features that contrast: a facial mismatch looks evil to us. The article gives an example of an actor with a round face and menacing eyebrows. The mismatch is unsettling and frightening to look at. Also, makeup artists may make a character look as if he or she is not exactly alive. The whole idea is to present a character who does not look the way a human being is supposed to look.[1]

When people look the way they are not supposed to look, we feel uncomfortable. When things aren't how they are supposed to be, we feel unsettled. We feel afraid.

Certainly Elijah must have felt as though something was "off." He was driven from his home when he opposed the evil king. After escaping the king, Elijah stood on the mountain as God commanded. There,

---

[1] (https://www.wsj.com/articles/the-secret-to-looking-sinister-on-screen-1502118703)

among the wind, the earthquake, the fire, and then the silence, there was nothing. Perhaps Elijah had been expecting a show of strength from God, but God showed up in just a voice, speaking to Elijah without all the commotion of thunder and flame.

Jesus' disciples were unsettled out on that boat in the middle of a storm. They thought they were seeing a ghost. Peter started walking on the water, but then realized there was a mismatch — hey wait a minute, I'm not supposed to be able to walk here.

But God conquers fear. Jesus says, take heart, it is I, do not be afraid. When things are off-kilter, unsettling, God conquers our fear. When there is nothing left but emptiness and silence, God conquers our fear.

The events in Charlottesville over the weekend are deeply unsettling, frightening, and hard to believe. Sinful beliefs that have plagued America through the generations, sinful beliefs such as white supremacy and bigotry, continue to haunt us. It's hard to believe that we see it again in 2017. But take heart ….

Many people believe that when fear is present, God is absent. Many people expect to find God when everything is calm and settled and in order. You can certainly find God when everything is going well. Yet God does amazing work when things are not right, unsettled, chaotic. In the midst of fear Jesus says, take heart, it is I, do not be afraid. In the midst of our fear, God comes, bringing new possibilities and new hope. God calls us to step out -- deliberately, faithfully, into that scary place.

Just a few moments before Peter stepped out onto the water, he thought he was seeing a ghost. Jesus conquered that fear. In that unreal moment, thinking it was a ghost, and realizing that God-With-Us was walking on the water, a new possibility sprang into Peter's mind. Perhaps he could walk on the water himself.

Jesus doesn't seem to mind this bold request. In fact, Jesus invited the disciples to ask for bold things. At another point Jesus encourages his disciples: "Very truly, I tell you, the one who believes in me will also do the works that I do and, in fact, will do greater works than these, because I am going to the Father. I will do whatever you ask in my name, so that the Father may be glorified in the Son. If in my name you ask me for anything, I will do it." (John 14:12 -14)

And when Peter began to fear, he began to doubt that his request to walk on water would truly be honored. When Peter doubted and feared, Jesus conquered that fear. He reached out and pulled Peter up. And apparently walked with Peter, on the water, back to the boat. So out of this fear came a new possibility — everyone on the boat worshiped Jesus as the Son of God.

What is our bold request today? Jesus has already said to us, take heart, it is I, do not be afraid.

What is our bold request for Charlottesville? Perhaps our bold request is for God to fulfill the prophecy in Revelation 21: 'See, the home of God is among mortals.

He will dwell with them;
they will be his peoples,
and God himself will be with them;
 he will wipe every tear from their eyes.
Death will be no more;
mourning and crying and pain will be no more,
for the first things have passed away.' (Rev. 21:3-4)

Are we willing to step out into the churning waters, confident that Jesus is there to guide us?

Today we are invited to ask for something bold ... for Charlottesville, and for people across the world. It just so happens that today, August 13, is a day to pray for reunification of the Korean peninsula. Even before the ratcheted-up rhetoric of recent days, the World Council of Churches declared today as a day of prayer for the peninsula, for reunification and for the churches and Christians there. Is that not a little unsettling? Just when I'm afraid because of what's on cable news, I'm called to pray. To step out in faith. Out of our fear, God hopes to create a new possibility.[2]

This prayer itself is brave. The prayer for Korea is stepping out in faith. Pray for the reunification of the Korean peninsula? Is that possible? Praying today, we are in solidarity with Korean families who continue to step out in faith, hoping to be reunited with family someday. Praying today, we are in solidarity with Christians in North Korea who step out in faith, daring

---

[2](http://www.oikoumene.org/en/press-centre/news/churches-across-the-world-invited-to-pray-for-korean-reunification)

to worship and serve. Praying today, we are in solidarity with soldiers who stand guard against danger, and diplomats who step out in faith, hoping to make progress against daunting odds.

Praying today for Charlottesville, we are in solidarity with the injured, with those who mourn, with law enforcement who worked hard to keep peace, with all who are bewildered and afraid. We boldly pray for a change of heart, in others and in ourselves too.

Surely in the face of danger and fear we can pray. If not, then we are indeed people of little faith. Surely when we are afraid, we can take at least one small step to make things better.

Clifton Kirkpatrick, the recent Stated Clerk of the Presbyterian Church (USA), writes about taking that small step in faith. He writes, "stepping out in faith is not a guarantee that we will not face troubled water or be filled with fear, but it is always accompanied by the assurance that Jesus will not abandon us, that when we need it most, he will extend his arm to lift us up and get us back in the boat." [3]

Let us pray. Holy God surround us with your steadfast love. Christ our Lord grant us your peace. Holy Spirit encourage us. Creator, Redeemer, Sustainer, help us to step out in faith with you. Amen.

---

[3] Kirkpatrick, Clifton. In *Daily Feast: Meditations from Feasting on the Word Year A,* edited by Kathleen Long Bostrom, Elizabeth F. Caldwell, and Jana K. Reiss (Louisville, KY: Westminster John Knox, 2013), 412.

Christ Is Present in Unlikely Places
Luke 2:1-20

Sacrament of Baptism (great-grandchild of our congregation's second-oldest member), Reception of New Member (mother of baptismal candidate)

Christmas Day 2016

Today, a Middle Eastern restaurant in London is offering free meal today to homeless and elderly who have no place to go for Christmas, or who cannot prepare their own meal.[4] The restaurant owners are Muslim but want to do something for their neighbors on this special day in the Christian calendar.

The restaurant owners thought of the event as a way to help the community and figured that 40 or 50 people would show up.

But then people heard about the idea and were moved and inspired by it. Word got around thanks to Facebook and some other social media. People began giving money to the restaurant so they could afford to give away food. And now there may be upwards of 500 people eating today.

If you want to look for Christ's presence in the world, look in the places where you least expect him to show up.

---

[4] https://www.bbc.com/news/uk-england-london-38218855

Look in a neighborhood restaurant … the owners follow one religion and the customers may follow another, or no religion at all. But none of that is as important as caring for others in the community.

Look in a field with shepherds watching over their flocks by night. Those watching the sheep lived their lives outdoors, not refined or well-groomed people, but important to God who wanted to announce a very special birth.

Look at a quiet moment with a humble man, and humble young woman, who had no idea what God was going to ask of them.

Look in a manger.

Among the sick and poor and neglected, Jesus is likely to show up.

Along a dusty road with weary travelers, you will find Jesus. In the sick room of a house, you will find Jesus. In a field teaching five thousand people, who had nothing to eat, you will find Christ our Lord.

And we may find the Christ child in other unexpected places, perhaps even among ourselves… you may have food to eat, but you may have a hungry spirit. You may have a roof over your head, but you have a heart that needs shelter. You may have Christmas lights in your home, but a certain dreariness in your soul. Although Jesus does show up at the end of his life in the halls of power, when he is on trial, most of the time he shows up among people who need food, or shelter, or healing, or who need light in their lives.

So may we follow the example of those who saw Jesus in unlikely places.

May we follow the example of the shepherds, who heeded the angels' call. After all, the angels didn't sing for King Herod or for Caesar. The angels sang for the shepherds and invited them to behold the child. May we follow like the wise men, who were from a foreign country and of a different religion but saw the light of the star and set out on their journey.

May we pay attention to the good happenings around us. May we be attentive and aware in those unlikely places, the places where poverty or suffering seem too shadowy and cloudy to let any light in.

And, when we see the Christ child, may we take time to worship and glorify God. I'm so glad we will celebrate the sacrament of baptism and welcome new member today, as a way to glorify God for the light in our lives, and in the life of these new members.

I will close with a prayer for Christmas from the Church of Scotland:

Today, O God, the soles of your feet have touched the earth. Today, the back street, the forgotten place has been lit up with significance. Today, the households of earth welcome the king of heaven. For you have come among us, you are one of us. So may our songs rise just around your throne as our knees bend to salute your cradle. Amen.[5]

---

[5] *A Book of Reformed Prayers* 1998 Westminster John Knox Press Lamar and Williamson

Part II:

Bloom Where You're Planted

Mental Health Month
Acts 11:1-18; Revelation 21:1-6

April 24, 2016

May is Mental Health Month.

At first glance it may seem that our Scriptures today are not about mental illness or any kind of illness or health. Today's Scriptures are from the lectionary, which is a schedule of readings used by many churches and developed decades ago. There are some passages in Scripture that could pertain to mental health — Scripture describes people who are brokenhearted, who feel out of control, who have poorly understood ailments. Today, I am interested in what our passage from Acts describes: a change of heart.

Today let's look at the change of heart, conversion even, that Peter experiences. Peter loved Jesus deeply. He wanted to be the best disciple ever, and because of his zeal, he was often given to excess. Sometimes he would just open his mouth and loudly declare whatever he was thinking, out of his love for God and God's son. Today we might say that someone like Peter has "no filter."

Sometime after the Resurrection, Peter receives a very specific call: a call to visit the Gentiles. Now Peter was a fisherman, not a religious scholar, but he loved the Lord. He didn't want to do anything to offend God or damage his relationship with the Lord. To him, the separation of Jews and Gentiles was still meaningful. To him, the laws of what to eat and what not to eat were very important in his life.

But the Holy Spirit was at work in Peter's heart, and in the hearts of many followers of Jesus. The Spirit was at work bringing people together … Giving everyone "the repentance that leads to life." (Acts 11:18)

So Peter receives a vision of animals that he believed were unclean, and was told, Kill and Eat. He was told to have fellowship with Cornelius, a Gentile and an officer in the Roman army, the army that occupied Peter's homeland … but Cornelius had come to learn about God and was well-respected in the Jewish community.

So Peter asks, who am I that I could hinder God? A good question for all of us to ask.

Today we make distinctions and make groups of "them" and "us." This happens particularly when we consider people living with mental illness. Those of us who believe we are well distance ourselves from those who are sick. When we have a family member or friend living with mental illness, we may experience a mixture of sympathy and confusion and maybe fear and maybe even anger … and that leads to separation … them versus us.

Churches in general, across America and across the globe, do little to minister to those living with mental illness. At a previous church I served, we had a prison ministry, and homebound communion, and gave some help to a nursing home serving low-income residents, but no help specifically for those living with a mental illness. In group homes, in homeless shelters, in Medicaid nursing homes, there are people living with mental illness.

I've been in ministry 15 years and the only specific mental illness outreach I've been involved in was a Christmas party for the inmates in a mental health unit of a prison. If it had not been for my uncle, who happened to be the chaplain of that prison, I don't know if I would have had that opportunity.

My uncle says that in the prison where he ministers, few of the inmates on the mental health unit get letters or commissary money from their families. Even fewer receive visits. Theirs is a lonely existence. At the brief Christmas party we held, many of them smiled and some shed tears.

We dance around this subject, mental illness. Whenever we share prayer concerns, we lift up prayers for surgeries, cancer treatment, safe travels, new jobs, loss of jobs, and a hundred other things, but we are never really sure how to bring up a prayer concern for mental illness.

Some people believe that sufferers of mental illness bring it on themselves. Or that they could cure themselves with enough prayer and faith. Some of us don't believe that, but we don't know exactly what to believe, or what to do.

Peter's experience shows how the Spirit of God moves into places where we don't know exactly what to do. Peter was certain that he was not supposed to eat with Gentiles or eat the Gentiles' food. Yet the Spirit moves when and where it wills. So Peter's ministry included a ministry to the Gentiles. Who would have guessed it? We cannot control the Holy Spirit.

God called Peter to visit outsiders, to go into a situation where Peter did not exactly know what to do. God called Peter to visit people whom Peter may have seen as deficient … lacking in faith… lacking in good judgment … lacking in morals. Peter saw God's work and saw that there was no distinction.

When we see someone with mental illness, do we judge them to be lacking? When we ourselves are diagnosed with a mental illness, do we view ourselves as deficient? I don't believe that's how God sees mental illness.

Revelation gives us a vision of a new heaven and a new earth, when every type of tear is wiped away. Even the tears we are reluctant to show to others. John's vision is a glimpse of God's larger vision.

What can we do, to show that there is no distinction? What can we do to help others see life? How can we repent, and be led to life? Here are some concrete things we can do to support those living with mental illness and their families:

— Use terms carefully. People joke and say they "feel bipolar," or I've heard people say that someone "went schizo." Let's be careful not to minimize or make jokes what is going on in people's real lives.

— Pray. At church we can pray for people living with mental illness, and we can mention those illnesses by name. Sometimes we don't feel comfortable naming the illness, and we say, please pray for so-and-so, who is going through a very rough time. That's OK too.

— Educate ourselves. I have an information table on mental illness for the month of May. Please take brochures.

— Learn what to watch out for. Feeling down for a short period of time happens to nearly everyone. For example, late in December, after the hubbub of Christmas, some people feel down. But when the down feeling persists, that's different and it needs professional care.

— Provide support! If your spouse or child or parent lives with mental illness, particularly a serious or difficult to treat mental illness, you are a caregiver. You pick up the slack, you remind your loved one of medications, you may even make appointments to see the mental health professional. Let's support our caregivers with prayer and with all the ways we normally support caregivers, with prayers and cards and food. Whether a loved one has been in the hospital for heart failure or has been in the ER for panic attacks or serious depression, a pan of lasagna is equally good.

There is no distinction between "them" and "us."

God's gift leads to life.

May we repent of keeping mental illness in the shadows. May we see things differently and allow the Spirit to shed light and give life.

Let us pray. O God, just as you have made your home among us, send us out to be among those who suffer. Tend to us in our own anxiety, depression, and confusing feelings. Help us repent of making distinctions between ourselves and others, even as you call those "others" to be your own. Wipe away every tear and bring us at last to your home among the saints in light.

Mary and Martha
Luke 10:38-42

July 21, 2019

I know many of you are busy. You are doers, helpers, and givers. You spend precious little time sitting down.

Thank you for what you do. Without you people would be hungry and thirsty, without shelter or clothing or a warm hug or listening ear. Your work is important. I fear that you may hear the story of Mary and Martha thinking that the kitchen work is unimportant, or unfaithful. The kitchen work, the background work, is a good work of faith.

You doers and helpers know an uncomfortable truth about your good works. Sometimes you are taken for granted.

Sometimes the givers give, and the takers take.

So you may find Jesus' words intriguing. What does Jesus mean by the part that will "not taken away from her?"

There were takers in Jesus' day and time too. The disciples had a bad habit of taking and not giving other people the chance to join in. They had good intentions, but they really did try to keep people away from Jesus! The disciples tried to block children … they tried to block a crowd of hungry people. Yet time and again, Jesus would give.

Jesus wanted to give to Martha. He wanted Martha in that room with everyone else listening to his teachings.

* * *

I knew a man who loved movies. Nights, weekends, he and his wife, or sometimes just he alone, were at a real theater watching the latest movies. He watched any and all kinds of movies. This man had a day job doing important work, but perhaps sometimes his work was routine or not particularly challenging. He had been in his profession over 30 years. His passion was the silver screen.

Hearing him talk about movies, it was apparent that being in the movie theater watching the show was a whole-body experience for him. He was immersed, engaged, absorbed.

That's how I see Mary: immersed and absorbed in God's presence.

You doers and helpers and givers ... you also need a time to immerse yourselves in God's presence. You need a time to sit at Jesus' feet. You are invited to have a seat in the circle with the disciples and friends of our Lord.

Why should you do this? A few reasons.

1. Jesus tells us not to worry. By worrying you will not add a single hour to your life. Sometimes you need to step away from your worries because your worries are not helping you.

2. There may come a day when you cannot do any more. Our ancestors worked and worked until the day they died. Today, many of us are given a gift our ancestors did not have: the gift of retirement, the gift of older age. Many of us — hear me out now — are given the gift of time laid up on the couch because we are 45 or 55 or 65, and not 25, and we pulled a muscle and it doesn't heal as quickly as it used to. When you are laid up, it's a time to pray, to rest, to accept others' help, to let someone do for you.

3. The third reason you should step away, immerse yourself in God's presence … is to guard against your very soul being taken away. If you give and give and give, and others take and take and take, there will be nothing of you left. God calls us to give — and God also calls us to receive.

Is it good to ignore the kitchen and the meals and the needs of the world? No, it is not good to ignore others' needs.

However— now is an opportune time in our society for everyone to sit at the table together. Lurking in the kitchen and grumbling will kill your spirit. Trying to get someone else to do for you will not get you anywhere. Come have a seat in the circle.

In kindergarten and first grade students have circle time. Everyone is in circle time — a student can sit beside her friends at circle, but she has to pay attention and participate. A student may not like anyone else in the class, but he has to attend.

And that's the better part— being together.

Let me say again - the work must be done, and people must eat. Yet it's also okay to take some time to sit with Jesus, to have fellowship with other people. It's okay for woman and man to sit in the fellowship circle together and then possibly work together on the meal. Jesus was a man, and he fed people! It's okay for Republicans and Democrats to sit at the same table. Actually, it is not acceptable when our elected representatives cannot get work done together. It is okay for Mary and for Martha to join the circle.

If we do not spend time with others in God's presence, how will we ever make any progress? We do ourselves no good when we are alone in the kitchen, angry and bitter.

Fellowship, spiritual growth, time with others, time enjoying God — these are all essential to our health. Indeed, without God's presence, life is a chore. Take time to be in God's presence. Take time to sit at Jesus' feet. Invite someone else to join the circle.

Thank you, workers and doers and helpers. Thank you, Lord, for the invitation to sit in your presence. I pray we will all accept Jesus' invitation. Amen.

The Prodigal Son
Luke 15:11-32

Fourth Sunday in Lent

March 10, 2013

(Note: this sermon is an imaginative retelling of Luke 15:11-32 from the Prodigal's perspective.)

There's Dad again, getting ready for a party. He loves parties and loves to see everyone having a good time.

You probably know my dad, and my whole family. Doubtless you've heard of me. I'm the one who had it all, and then threw it all away.

I don't know why I did it. I had everything I needed, and I took it for granted. When I think back my face gets flushed and my heart beats faster -- I feel a sense of panic. I don't ever want to be totally alone like that again.

I should have seen it coming -- when my money ran out, the so-called friends vanished. What was I thinking, that I could buy friendship or love?

Sometimes I wonder if God sent the famine. I was already in dire straits when my money ran out, and the famine pushed things to the extreme. But maybe without the famine I never would have come to my senses.

Anyway, I don't really know why I came back. Some people say I should have just died over there with the pigs. That is what I deserved, but something moved me to try.

Now, when I see Dad, and watch him getting excited about the party, ordering the servants about and fussing over food, I remember the day I came back. I wasn't able to speak from the heart that day, it hurt too much. I wasn't that brave — I guess I'm not really a brave man. Plus I knew I had violated the all rules about how a son should relate to his father.

So I made a speech. "Father, I have sinned against heaven and against you. I am not worthy to be called your son. Please treat me as one of your hired hands." And I rehearsed it.

Well, he came running toward me, as other people sneered and made snide remarks, and my heart stopped. All I could do was continue my speech. And he embraced me, and I felt so loved and so miserable all at the same time.

Dad is so loving, and what I admire about him is that he doesn't care what anybody thinks. He is brave. He just wants to share, and he wants everyone to love one another. I wish I could be that way.

Oops! Did I forget telling you what this party today is all about? My brother is getting married. There he is, getting ready for the party. I think he looks happy.

I hope he knows how much Dad loves him. When we had that huge embarrassing party for me, Dad actually left the party to go see if he was all right.

I know I annoyed my brother in the past. He's so responsible, and I'm, well ... you know.

I'm not on speaking terms with my brother, for the umpteenth time. A couple weeks ago my brother came back from a meeting with his future father-in-law and he was at it again, whining about how no one appreciates him. I said, you're a lucky man, you're marrying the most beautiful girl in the village from one of the best families. How could you complain? You always complain about people not appreciating you. We're pretty darn fortunate and blessed by God to be born into a rich house. You have everything you need, stop whining. I hope you won't treat your beautiful fiancée that way.

I told him exactly what I thought. And I don't care if I offended him. I'm keeping clear of him for a while, but I believe I spoke the truth. I know now all there is to know about being grateful and being open to grace.

Don't get me wrong, I don't feel superior to him or to anybody. I just know what I know, and I learned it the hard way.

I wish I could get married. That banquet was supposed to restore me to good graces, but honestly, no father in the village will talk to me about marriage with his daughter. I might have to leave again. Sometimes I wish I didn't have everyone watching me the way they do now.

I don't know what I'll do. It would have been much easier to just be a hired hand -- eat and sleep with the servants and live out my days here. I think I would have even been willing to serve my brother after Dad goes. I would have had my daily needs met that way, just a quiet life in the servants' quarters.

But now I'm a full brother again, and I have all these responsibilities: take care of Dad, work hard on the farm, Dad says I have to get married and start a family -- it's a lot of work. I have a lot of catching up to do.

Even though I don't feel up to the task, Dad believes I can do it.

I don't know what will happen to our farm and our land in the future. People talk about how I "squandered my inheritance" – well, what I did was, I took my land and sold it. I can't believe I did that, but that's what I did. The lovely vineyard over there on the hill was mine to inherit from Dad, and I sold it. Anyway, Dad is looking into buying it back, so that my brother will have all *his* original land and not have to divide it further with me. I told Dad, I meant what I said about being a hired hand. Let me be and leave the land thing alone -- but he won't hear of it.

I will accept whatever happens. As it is, I am grateful for every breath of air, every morsel of food, every drop of clean water. And I mean that.

I've gotta run, time for the party. I'm going to be quiet, not eat too much or drink too much, be very kind and polite to everyone. Wish me well! I need all the prayers I can get.

Honoring One Another
1 Samuel 1:4-20, Mark 13:1-8

November 18, 2018

The polarized political discourse has been on everyone's minds lately. It's on TV, in print news … it even came up at Bible study recently. Lately we have been asking — How can we repair the breach in our society? How can we talk with one another, live with one another, even approach one another?

Let's start with a story.

There was a young man who left home to seek his fortune. He began his quest around the year 1950. He left home, got a job in a city far away. He fell in love. By the time the young man's mother was able to make the trip to visit him, the young man and his sweetheart had already begun a family.

The mother arrived at her son's small apartment in the big city. She surveyed the apartment and its residents. Here was the young lady with whom her son was in love: Mom had never met her. The young couple wore wedding bands, but Mom had not attended any wedding. Here was the toddler, all bright eyes and chubby legs. Mom had no idea she had become a grandmother. Mom faced a choice. What's a mother to do?

Mom decided to honor her son and his family. She held the little child. She kissed her son. She said, "You have a beautiful family." She went home, still a little surprised at all these developments, but happy. Her son had a purpose in life ... he had loving relationships ... and Mom knew, those things mean a lot. Maybe things had progressed in a way Mom had not envisioned for her son. Yet, she honored her son's love and work and family.

How do we repair the breach?

* * *

In the household of Elkanah, there is dishonor. Peninnah has children, Hannah does not. Peninnah is what we might call today a troll — she wants to make sure Hannah is reminded, often, of her own unhappiness.

There is so much possible pain and possible dishonor around the issue of children: not being able to have any, having fewer than you would like, having more than people think is "proper," health in danger because of pregnancy complications, miscarriages, pregnancies early in life, pregnancies late in life, troubles in parenting. And the list goes on. A Bible professor, Kathryn Schifferdecker, notes: "as anyone who has dealt with the profound pain of infertility knows, all words are insufficient.... There is a place in this story for lament."[6]

---

[6] (http://www.workingpreacher.org/preaching.aspx?commentary_id=3857)

We get pretty darn judgmental over women and their pregnancies or lack of pregnancy. Women judge themselves over issues of pregnancy and parenting.

Back to today's reading. There is dishonor in this house where poor Hannah lives. The head of household, Elkanah, is sweet and caring but unsure what to do.

So Hannah takes her dishonor to God. When the time for the worship at the temple comes, she prays so fervently that the priest thinks something is wrong with her. When he finds out about her pain, the old priest Eli honors that pain and those tears. May God grant your request, he says.

There is something powerful and true in honoring someone else's story.

Our reading today is a precursor to Christmas Scripture readings, which are coming up soon. Hannah is a model for Mary, the mother of Jesus — a humble woman who trusts God, a strong woman who knows God will do what is right. Hannah sings a song:

He raises up the poor from the dust;
  he lifts the needy from the ash heap,
to make them sit with princes
  and inherit a seat of honour.
For the pillars of the earth are the Lord's,
  and on them he has set the world. (1 Samuel 2:8)

And Mary sings a song:

He has brought down the powerful from their thrones, and lifted up the lowly;
  he has filled the hungry with good things,
    and sent the rich away empty. (Luke 1:52-53)

Do you hear the similarities? God raises up those who are dishonored. God gives the lowly good things.

This story is about God stepping into our pain and walking with us through it. This is about God helping us overcome shame that the world heaps on us. This is about God honoring a person and helping her find purpose in her life. This is about God bringing honor to places of dishonor.

Also, our reading from Mark is a precursor to Christmas — it's about tearing down dishonor in the world. Last week we read about a poor lady who put all she had into the treasury of the temple, whereas rich people put in large sums. She has hope for something good to come of her small offering — and it seems no one acknowledges her contribution except for Jesus. So the dishonor of the poor and vulnerable built into those walls will come down. Jesus comes to be the Wonderful Counselor, the Prince of Peace, the one who lifts up the lowly and fills them with good things.

We will make progress in two ways: one, if we have a life full of good things, even if we've had some letdowns, we can honor the lowly, the forgotten, the hungry. Two, if we find ourselves lowly or forgotten or hungry, we can honor others, not by lashing out, but by taking our pain to God.

We can help raise people up from shame and dishonor.

What impresses me about Hannah is this — she wants God to expand the honor, to include her. I don't think she wants to take away anything from Peninnah to dishonor the one who dishonored her. Hannah just wants the pie to be larger, so she can have a piece.

Today our cultural divides are framed in terms of win-lose, or in terms of a limited amount of pumpkin pie.

We cannot make progress if we think in terms of win-lose. But God can work through us if we are open to the idea of a win-win, a larger pie, a pie big enough for everyone to have a piece.

I believe we will do well if we honor one another. Honoring one another's accomplishments, and sincere pain — not just gripes but sincere pain — can help us repair the breach.

We will do well if we bring our own shame, dishonor and pain before God. Not hoping to get someone else back for what they have done to us but praying for God to do something good with us.

May we honor others. May we honestly bring our pain before God. May we allow God to do good things through us. Amen.

Falling in Love
Luke 5:1-11

February 10, 2019

Some people love Valentine's Day. Some people think the day is too commercialized and mushy. But Valentine's Day does give me an excuse for what I hoped would be a catchy title for a sermon on love.

Those first disciples fell in love with Jesus. Really? Fell in love? Yes. In Deuteronomy, we are encouraged to love the Lord your God with all your heart, with all your mind, and with all your soul. Here we read about a moment of falling in love with God, totally and completely.

Are fisherman romantic? I don't know. It seems there is a certain romance with the sea. I know fishermen are practical. When these practical people heard Jesus, advice to go back out there and try again, they must have thought Jesus was being ridiculous. Practical people would not do something ridiculous.

Love is ridiculous. It causes us to jump head over heels. It causes us to pledge our lives in marriage to another human being. Love challenges us to go back and try again when there has been a tempest of a temper tantrum, or a gloomy cloud of grumpiness, or lightning flashes of hot emotion.

Love is ridiculous ... but it is the stuff we are made of. It is in our very bones. God loves this world, of which we are a part. For God so loved the world that he gave his only begotten son… The one we worship and know in our hearts is love. In first John we read, God is love.

Would you like to fall in love with God again? Would you like to fall in love with God's world again?

* * *

Candice Payne paid for hotel rooms for the homeless in her city, to get them out of this extreme winter weather. Other people found out about her effort and contributed. In total, she helped 120 people stay safe and warm. In one interview, she minimized her accomplishment, saying I'm just a girl from the South Side. Just a person who felt love in her heart and wanted to do something. One could say Ms. Payne was in love with her city, in love with God's world, and her love led to a giant act of kindness.[7]

Let me take a step back here. I'll be the practical fisherman for a moment. I know we cannot save the world on the credit cards of kind people.

I know we don't always feel love. I know we get hurt sometimes. Some of Jesus' disciples hurt him. At one point his disciples got into an argument, most likely hurting one another in the process.

I know we get tired sometimes. Even Jesus attempted to take some time away to rest.

---

[7] (https://wgntv.com/2019/02/07/woman-who-helped-find-shelter-for-homeless-during-polar-vortex-gets-50k-on-ellen-show/)

And yet, we long to hear that voice of love... that voice calling us to wake up, to try again, to believe.

We long to hear again the story of God's love.

I believe a lot of hurting people out there would love to hear a love story. I believe a lot of folks would like to be part of a love story. They have fished all night and have come up empty. Somewhere, somehow, they need to hear God's encouragement to try again.

Falling in love with God might feel like...

— an inspiration
— an impetus to do something
— knowing God when you see God
— knowing something important when you see it

Unless you enjoy fishing with a net in the middle of the night, you may not have a love story exactly like the one we read today. So then, what is your love story? What is the story of your love for God, and God's love for you? Think about that story and share it.

The world is waiting to hear how you fell in love.

Let us pray. Lord, when you call us, may we respond with our whole heart. May we love you with all our heart, all our soul, all our mind, and all our strength, just as you love us. Amen.

Bloom Where You're Planted
Jeremiah 29:1, 4-7; Luke 17:11-19

October 13, 2013

At the last church I served, the senior pastor position was shared for a while by a husband and wife. They were co-pastors. The husband often described the wife as someone who "blooms where she's planted."

He was right. That particular husband and wife had endured a lot together. She faced discrimination as a woman in ministry. They both went through the distress of having a child diagnosed with a serious medical condition, and the nonstop work of finding good care for that child. Many times during their marriage, the husband would find a church and the wife would be "the trailing spouse," finding church work after moving into the new community.

Jeremiah writes to his beloved people who had endured a lot together. Jeremiah's people were Jews in exile. Many of his beloved people had been carried off to Babylon, as part of a regime change plan by the Babylonian empire. Babylon broke up conquered nations by carrying off the elite and trying to incorporate them into the Babylonian elite. Politically, an innovative strategy -- conquer by enticing everyone to become like you.

Yet in their captivity, the Jewish people found a way to live their lives. They stayed and built a life and a community for themselves but maintained a separate identity from the surrounding culture. Some did enjoy the creature comforts of the elite life, and we have some indications that some were willing to compromise their heritage and their teachings. Others were not willing to give in and become full Babylonian. Those who did not give in knew what they did not want to do but wondered what to do. Jeremiah wrote to them, build your life. Do not waste away with mourning. Don't forget where you came from but do remember that God has a future planned for you. Bloom where you're planted.

Many of us have experienced the sensation of being in exile, suddenly swept out of our usual lives and placed in unknown circumstances. The recession, a sudden illness -- circumstances can move you to a place you've never been before, where you don't know the language or how to get along, and you are faced with a limited range of choices. When you are in exile, you can crumple under your grief, or get going and build a new life for yourself in a new land.

What I'm describing is not easy. Wouldn't it be wonderful if God could erase everything, and take us back to the days before? The days before the pink slip. The days before the word "cancer" emerged from the doctor's mouth. The days before ... The days when everyone knew his place or her place, and knew all their neighbors, and sat behind the same lady with the same hat in the same pew every Sunday. Wouldn't it be wonderful if we didn't have to go to these new places where we have to build lives for ourselves out of what seems like nothing?

If we go to the new place, blessings are waiting there too. Blessings that help us bloom. Think about the lepers cured in the Gospel story. All of these people had been in exile due to their disease. Nine of them went back to things as they were before. Before the dreaded diagnosis. Yet one leper decided to stay, just for a little while. He returned to give thanks, and he received a blessing from Jesus. "Go in peace. Your faith has made you well."

We don't know what else happened that day. The former lepers may have gone home and built vineyards and hewed cisterns and married or had children. They may have blossomed after their cure. Yet I admire the way the one former leper decided to hold on to the moment just a little longer. We may have witnessed in him a blooming of faith, a blooming of a completely new life.

May we bloom where we are planted. May we go in peace. May our faith make us well.

Home by Another Way
Matthew 2:1-12

Epiphany Sunday
Ordination and Installation of Ruling Elders

January 7, 2018

So many people in Scripture took a journey that did not take the route they had imagined. Jacob, Abraham, Naaman, perhaps Mary and Joseph. Paul. The magi.

Today I'd like to focus on the last verse of this passage: "they left for their own country by another road."

For the magi, the going home was just as important as the arrival, and the time spent giving gifts and praising God. After all, how would they tell about their journey, if they never completed the trip back home?

Think about what it meant at that time to take a different road. There were not as many options for travel as we have today. No interstate networks. No hotels with free wifi. Bandits and thieves lurked by the roadways, hoping to relieve traders of their goods and money.

On that journey the magi discovered something:

A different road can still lead you home.

So many times we find ourselves on an unexpected journey, or a different road. Not the road we thought we would take. And we wonder where this new road leads.

Some may say, I don't know how to go home to my family anymore. My family has changed. In fact, the feeling of "home" is just about gone. It isn't the same since Mom passed away, since the kids grew up, since my friends are gone. Home can change but still be the same. A home in Ireland is so old that when they turned over one of the steppingstones, because it had a groove worn in it from so many feet over the years, they found that the other side had the same groove! Generations may come and go but the steppingstone still leads to the front door. The home is still a home.

Some people say this church feels like home. And then it may feel jarring to realize that others in your home do not agree with you on some very important questions. Let me ask you — in your own home, or in the home in which you grew up, did everyone agree? We just celebrated Christmas and some of you may have spent some time with relatives. If your family is anything like my family, you voted differently in 2016, you attend different types of churches, you have a variety of opinions on all kinds of things. If there is disagreement around the dinner table at Grandma's house, does it mean that Grandma's house is no longer home? I don't think so.

So I believe our faith community can still be home. We may simply need to approach our home by another road. My mentor Bill Neely was able to invite a lot of people "home." He was active in civil rights work in South Carolina decades ago. For that reason, various white church members were displeased with him, or didn't understand his passion for civil rights. But those same white church members would still go to breakfast with Bill and he would still go to their hospital room and their daddy's funeral and all the important events in their lives.

Today we ordain and install our elders. Trust our elders and officers of the church to lead us home. Our elders are hard at work making sure we have lunches, like our potluck lunch today, and other fellowship opportunities, so we can sit around the table with one another, the way people do at home. Our elders are hard at work providing for our educational opportunities, so we can think in a spiritual sense about the world around us. Our elders spend time in prayer and discussion when a tough issue presents itself — the way that mothers and fathers and grandparents and caregivers pray and consider issues affecting the family and the home.

Finally, this year I encourage all of us to think about what road we are traveling, in a spiritual sense, in order to lead us home. Who are our traveling companions on this road? I'm afraid we all spend too much time in what is called "outrage culture" — that is, spending too much time watching cable news, and looking at social media and websites, that are trying to grab our attention. And the way cable news or social media grabs our attention is giving us something to be outraged, offended, fired up about. Herod was a good example of outrage culture — he felt threatened, offended, and flew into a rage. Now it's good to have some fire in your belly from time to time. But not when the fire consumes you.

Consider this year adding a daily Scripture reading as your traveling companion. Consider adding some time spent in silence as your traveling companion. Take some time every day to consider how God is present with you - the very same God who walks with you through the valley of the shadow of death and leads you to green pastures and still waters. Cable news takes you to a fiery place and leaves you there — but God guides us and protects us on a different road.

Trust that God will provide that new road in the face of threats to body, mind, and spirit. Trust that the light of Christ will be there to lead you on your way to your destination and back again.

Listen to God's voice in Scripture, in hymns, in Sunday school and in worship, even in dreams — and trust that God's Spirit will lead you home.

Let us pray. God, help us receive your light, brought into the world in your infant Son Jesus Christ. Help us to live in that light. Help us when we travel on a new road and remind us that you are there to guide us. Amen.

Part III

You've Got This

Hope in a Clay Jar
2 Corinthians 4:5-12

June 3, 2018

Dr. Steve Hayner was one of my teachers and mentors in my doctoral program. I was greatly influenced by Steve's words and advice through the years. I was not alone.

Steve became ill about four years ago. He was diagnosed with pancreatic cancer. The fact that he was sick hurt many people. How could he be sick? Suddenly the person so many depended upon was not in the office, not able to answer emails or phone calls asking for advice. Losing someone you depend on hurts and losing your access to someone you depend on is unsettling to say the least.

Some of the early Christians depended heavily upon Paul, and when he was away, or unable to make a return visit, doubt would creep into their minds. Even more unsettling — there was something about Paul's physical condition that bothered people. We don't know exactly what it was, but doubt would creep in when people considered his condition. How could a man of God be physically imperfect, even sick? Certain antagonists took advantage of people's doubt.

Yet God is a God of hope, even in the most trying of circumstances. Hope when our body is weak. Hope when we don't see results, we wanted to see. Hope when we experience setbacks or roadblocks.

Steve signed up for the website Caring Bridge, which helps people in many ways. On Caring Bridge the sick person, and family members, can write updates. People can send a note of encouragement. And other services are offered. Anyway, Steve wrote about being faithful each day, even as his body became weaker. Each day, he writes, has a calling. Even if the calling is just to appreciate the care you are receiving from medical staff, friends and family, that is a call to learn more about gratitude.

Now some people were disappointed in Steve's idea that each day had a calling. They wanted stories of miraculous healing, powerful prayers that lifted their spirits, something monumental from the man who, in their opinion, was larger than life. Kind of like how some people were disappointed in Paul.

Paul's witness is this: hope can come in a clay jar. Hope may arrive on the wings of eagles, in the voice of an angel, in the raising of the dead ... yet hope can also be found as God works through our regular everyday selves, weak as those selves may be.

In fact, our weakness makes hope all the more powerful. God can do extraordinary things with an ordinary life. So.... Is there a reason for his suffering? For Paul, there is a reason. Hear again verse 7 from the passage we read:

But we have this treasure in clay jars, so that it may be made clear that this extraordinary power belongs to God and does not come from us.

Of course God can show power however God chooses. Some people say we need death and suffering in order to appreciate life.... we need night in order to appreciate day ... and I'm not sure that is the case. What I am saying is that we are made mortal. Our bodies will break down and we will die. But in that there is a gift... even in the mortal body God's eternal light can shine. Even in the jar made of clay there is an everlasting treasure. You may have heard it said, God don't create no junk. So the clay jar, the mortal body, it is all good in God's eyes.

Allow me to quote to you from Steve's website — this time a reflection from Steve's daughter Emilie Wagner, who was struggling to explain her father's condition to her children —

I find myself repeating this ever-important truth to my kids and to myself: death hurts because we were made for life. "I have set before you life and death," we read in Deuteronomy 30: 19. "Choose life." Some would say that "choosing life" means choosing only to see the positive, looking always for the silver lining. To walk this path is to live in perpetual denial. Following Jesus means choosing to see the truth even when it is painful. Death hurts. Loss causes deep ache. And somehow in the agony of pain, we are free to find joy because we can trust that Jesus redeems all things. Where death reminds us that we are made of dust, inconsequential in the course of history, Jesus reminds us that in him we are loved and have life forever. That is a reason to sing even on dark days. For me, choosing life means asking hard questions about suffering. Choosing life means admitting I'm angry and brokenhearted. Although I could avoid the grief and teach my children to do the same, this would be a mistake.

The path of freedom, I think, is to look death square in the eyes and proclaim, "I choose life."[8]

Death can be at work in us, or in people we love. But life can be at work at the same time. God says, let light shine out of darkness, and God means it.

Don't give up hope because clouds or shadows creep in. Don't give up hope if the flame on the candle flickers. Don't give up on the vessel just because it is made of clay.

Instead, place your hope in the redeeming power of Jesus Christ. Place your hope in the goodness of God's creation. Place your hope in the comfort and courage provided by the Holy Spirit. Place your hope in God, who has shone in our hearts to give the light of the knowledge of the glory of God in the face of Jesus Christ.

Let us pray. In a world filled with doubt, O Lord, let us trust in your extraordinary power. Grant us a peace that the world cannot give but can be found only through Jesus Christ our Lord. Amen.

---

[8] Steve and Sharon Hayner, *Joy in the Journey: Finding Abundance in the Shadow of Death* (Downers Grove, IL: InterVarsity Press, 2015), 85, Kindle.

Life Finds a Way
John 20:1-18

Easter Sunday
April 1, 2018

(Note for reader: our early Easter service begins at the columbarium, often with Mark 16:1-8. The rest of the service takes place in the sanctuary.)

"For they were afraid." So ends the Easter story in Mark, as we read at the columbarium.

The women found themselves in an unexpected place. They thought the tomb be a sad place and had most likely prepared themselves to be sad.

They had prepared to be in a place of death but there, at the tomb, they found life.

Other disciples found life too. Other disciples saw the tomb that morning, or saw Jesus in the first Easter evening, or encountered Jesus in the days following.

One of the great truths of Easter is this ...

Life finds a way. God finds a way to bring life where we thought there was only death.

I found a symbol of new life this week: a rock with grass growing out of crevices. Let me be clear, plants grow out of crevices in rocks all the time. You may have seen entire trees growing on the slimmest ledge. But this time, I was out looking for rocks without plants on them: rock rocks. We plan to paint rocks with encouraging messages in Sunday school today. I was looking for rocks with no signs of life, and when I stumbled upon the one rock with grass bursting forth from it, I stopped. I even took pictures of it. We may be looking for death, but life finds a way.

Life finds a way ...

> — in the midst of betrayal
> — in the midst of abandonment
> — in the midst of fear
> — in the midst of worry and diminished hope

Life can find a way into the heart of someone bent on death and destruction. Paul writes about the good news being revealed to him, as to someone untimely born— he was bent on destroying followers of Jesus.

Will we allow betrayal or fear to be the end of the story?

You can try to wall yourself off against fear, or betrayal. But then there is no life in you.

Remember you don't need to be a rock. Jesus is our rock, Peter is the rock of the church, but the rest of us simply need to rely on the solid rock of Christ.

Jesus is our rock - and we can rest on him.

The rock provides some foundation — you can build on it, build a place of life and faith such as this church here. You can rest on it. If you're a blade of grass or a sliver of moss or even a sapling of a tree, you may be able to root yourself in that rock.

And remember the rock is rolled away ... rolled away to make room for life.

So where will life find a way in your life? Where will the new life in Christ be real for you?

You may find new life in reconciliation, forgiveness of past misdeeds and making amends. You may find new life in renewed hope, allowing yourself to hope for something you'd given up on. You may find new life in a new awareness of God's presence.

Where we may be expecting only death, God provides life.

Life finds a way, and for that, we are grateful.

Hope Does Not Disappoint
Romans 5:1-5

June 16, 2019

Everything in the Bible paints a picture.

Sometimes the Bible teaches what *should be*. Sometimes it paints a picture of the way things *are* — the Bible encourages us to look and listen and learn. Sometimes the Bible paints a picture of the way things *could be* — it teaches us to hope in the future.

When we read a passage, we have to consider what the point of this passage is.

Please, do not take Romans 5:1-5 and read it as text telling you what you *should* do.

Let me explain — who here has ever felt at your wit's end? Like you've tried everything, and nothing works? The last thing you need, in that situation, is someone telling you what you should do. Say you have a nervous habit, like nail biting, and say right now you are going through a particularly nerve-wracking time. As a result, your nails are chewed up and ragged. Would it be helpful for someone to remind you, now don't bite your nails! Would that help? Probably not.

So do not read this passage as instruction on how you *should* act. (wagging my finger) Now be good when you're suffering, fight hard, suffering is good for your character!

Allow me to paraphrase these verses and read this passage to you a different way. I compared our reading to some other Bible translations and came up with this-

Yes, you are suffering. Your suffering will produce endurance - in other words, you will find that you have what you need to make it through each day. You will make it through each moment as it comes. Your endurance will produce character — in other words, you will not crack or fall apart. You will be tested but you will make it through. Your character will produce hope, and hope does not disappoint us, because God's love has been poured into our hearts through the Holy Spirit that has been given to us.

So Paul paints a picture of how things *could* be. How God desires the world to be.

Paul gives us even more in this passage, as he paints a picture of God's care for us.

Notice other key words in this passage — faith, peace, glory, rejoice, hope, love

Does anyone have an awareness ribbon or T-shirt or bracelet? You know how you can get a pink ribbon for breast cancer awareness, a red ribbon for AIDS awareness, green is for mental illness.

If you or someone you love is dealing with one of these illnesses, do not feel like you have to be a warrior every day. Even warriors rest. Use the ribbon as a symbol of hope. Use the ribbon or T-shirt as a reminder of hopes and dreams for the future.

Last week my daughter and I did our nails. She got the idea that I should have one nail painted a different color. So we chose navy blue. Now our navy-blue nail polish did not have any particular meeting. But one member of our congregation did have fingernail polish with a meaning. When he was going through stem cell transplants, he had one orange nail for leukemia awareness. I admired his sense of hope and joy.

The Bible paints a picture for us. Today, let these words paint for you a picture of hope and joy. *Hope does not disappoint us, because God's love has been poured into our hearts through the Holy Spirit that has been given to us.* Thanks be to God.

The Call, the Cry, the Answer
Isaiah 58:1-12

(This sermon was preached for an Ash Wednesday service held jointly by two congregations, the one I serve and the other in a nearby town.)

Prayer before sermon:

Jesus, remember us when you come into your kingdom. Hear our prayers.

For your church around the world, we ask new life. For all who carry out ministries in your church, we ask grace and wisdom.

For people who have accepted spiritual disciplines, we ask inspired discipleship.

For Christians of every land, we ask new unity in your name.

For Jews and Muslims and people of other faiths, we ask your divine blessing.

For those who cannot believe, we ask your faithful love.

For governors and rulers in every land, we ask your guidance.

For people who suffer and sorrow, we ask your healing peace.

Holy God, your Word, Jesus Christ, spoke peace to a sinful world and brought humanity the gift of reconciliation by the suffering and death he endured. Teach those who bear his name to follow the example he gave us. May our faith, hope, and charity turn hatred to love, conflict to peace, and death to eternal life; through Christ our Lord. Amen.

Ash Wednesday is our day. Lent is our time.

I wonder about other seasons of the church: whether those other seasons really belong to the church anymore! Christmas got away from us a long time ago. Easter seems to have gotten away from us as well. We are just as familiar with the Easter bunny as we are with the empty tomb.

Christians are more and more claiming Lent as our time, for our faith. In the past several years I have noticed a lot more people paying attention to the season of Lent. It's on social media. Creative types have come up with all kinds of artwork to use in churches or at home, and hands-on activities for children during Lent. Our Director of Christian Education made a bulletin board for Lent with a road leading to a cross. On the road are written words such as Pray, Remember, Love — in total there are 40 letters in the words she wrote, symbolizing the 40 days of Lent. Christians are making this season their own.

I hope no one ever makes a commercial enterprise out of Lent. So far, the only commercial aspect I've seen is the grocery store advertising fish, for those who are staying away from meat during Lent. This is our time, our time of prayer and preparation.

Why do we have this time, our time? Because what we do is not all about ourselves. We are God's people. We need this time to remind ourselves who we are, and whose we are.

So, I'm going to take back what I said at the beginning of the sermon. Sort of. Ash Wednesday is not really our day, it's God's day. Lent is not really our time, it's God's time. We belong to God, we are saved through Christ, we are called by the Holy Spirit, and this is our time—the time—God's time … to claim who we are, and whose we are.

Today we are called to be Christ's people not for ourselves. We are called to be Christ's people for the benefit of the entire world.

This prayer we just used is from the Presbyterian Church (USA) Book of Common Worship. In this book, there are several prayers included for goodwill and blessing for people of other faiths, or of no faith. Those prayers are in the book for a reason. Our faith is not a private possession, something we use for our own good feelings. Our faith is present for the benefit of God's entire creation. We are to be a people of blessing for the world: people who do God's work of sharing bread with the hungry, loosening the bonds of injustice, breaking the yokes of abuse and addiction and poverty and discrimination.

Today, if you choose to accept ashes on your head, accept them for the world. Accept spiritual discipline, such as prayer, and reading Scripture, for the world. The world needs people like you and me who say we are faithful to be faithful. The world needs people who say they believe in love to be loving. The world needs people who profess a belief in new life, eternal life, to offer ... life.

The world cries out and calls to God, using different names and different forms of religious expression. Using our own form of expression, let us present a fast acceptable to God. Let us engage in ministries of mercy, justice, compassion, and help.

Isaiah calls the people away from fasting and worship that is focused on the self. Perhaps there was an element of people feeling good about themselves because they were so good at fasting and self-denial. Some people today feel proud, maybe a little too proud, when they stick to a strict diet or carry out an intense exercise regimen. Lent is not about being strict with one's self in the service of pride or self-image. Lent is about God's time and God's work. Isaiah calls the people to be like God, who says, "Here I am" when God's people call. May we use those words ourselves — here I am — when we see the world around us.

During this season of Lent, let us make good use of God's time, and our time. God has chosen an acceptable fast. May our ashes, our prayers, our spiritual disciplines, all point the way to God's call. May our ashes, our prayers, our spiritual disciplines, all point toward those who cry out. May our ashes, our prayers, our spiritual disciplines, remind us to call on God for help — and God will say, you called, and here I am. Thanks be to God.

A Life of Love
1 Corinthians 13

February 3, 2019

One thousand. Some said two thousand. Some said five thousand.

Last week, the call went out to attend the funeral of a veteran who appeared to have no family. Cars lined up on the road to the cemetery to say goodbye to him and give him military honors. The attendance was staggering. As many as 5000 people were there. [9]

* * *

Love bears all things … endures all things … hopes all things.

Some of the Christians in the city of Corinth, from which we get the name Corinthians, were, in a way, similar that veteran in Texas. Invading forces burned the city about 150 years before the birth of Christ — they killed off the population or sold them into slavery. So the new city was a Roman colony, a mix of people from all over the Roman Empire. People far from home, just like the veteran Joseph Walker was far from his family and home.

---

[9] https://www.npr.org/2019/01/28/689378272/after-hearing-u-s-veteran-had-no-family-huge-crowd-attends-his-funeral-in-texas

Paul wrote to this diverse group of people about how they should get along with one another: not to boast, or be arrogant, or rude. Not to become enamored of themselves, feeling that they are better than others in the group. Not to get irritable or hold grudges.

Paul wrote to them about what he called "still a better way," and by that he means ... love.

* * *

Seventy thousand — that's the amount of dollars raised by an eleven-year-old girl. [10]

An eleven-year-old girl got bored at the nursing home where her mother worked. It was a home for Medicaid patients, meaning people with very little money. Medicaid pays for the patients' room and board. Medicaid barely provides for personal care, such as a haircut, shampoo, a new pair of pajamas every so often. Families are supposed to pick up the tab for personal care and for little extras, but there may be no family. The family may be strapped for cash too. And, sometimes, the family seems not to care.

So the girl asked residents what they would like. Residents responded with simple requests ... fresh fruit ... a book to read ... someone to feed the cats that hang out in the home's yard. The residents enjoyed watching the cats.

---

[10] https://www.cnn.com/2019/01/29/health/iyw-5th-grader-nursing-home-mission-trnd/index.html

One resident wanted to help with the project ... talking to others about how they are feeling, what they need. It lifted her spirits to do something for someone else.

This is the type of love Paul writes about. In Greek it's called agape. A selfless love, a giving love, a love that puts others interests first.

Love is going to be what saves us from ourselves. I'm not talking about romantic love or friendship love. I'm talking about agape, the love that inspires you to get up and do something.

* * *

There are three kinds of people who enter a Medicaid nursing home.

— the first kind are those who actually don't enter, because they don't want to see illness or death. Or they don't have time. Or they think someone else will do it.

— the second kind are those who do go in, but then begin to run their mouth: complaining about how the place smells. Wondering how all those pitiful people got in that condition. Saying somebody ought to do something about the place.

— then there's the third kind. People who enter and show love.

What is love in a Medicaid nursing home? Listening. Learning people's names. Getting to know people. Getting past yourself, putting this vulnerable and forgotten person who is sitting across from you first. Most of the time, with forgotten people, somebody ought to do something. And that person is you. The government has done its job — the payments went out, and the nursing home has been inspected by the county. The family may be poor, and they do what they can, or maybe they don't do anything at all. But if you go in, you are the somebody who needs to do something — and that something is love.

Who gets up early in the morning and drives to a funeral for someone they have never met?

There are those who don't attend funerals.
There are those who say somebody ought to do something — the VA should have done better, or the family should have done this or that. Some of the family of that veteran did come forward. Who knows, maybe they had lost contact with him over the years.

I think we ought to ask our leaders about whether they show love. We should ask them; do you go to funerals? Do you meet with people who never get visitors? Do you give of yourself?

Our world is full of people who trumpet their accomplishments. Our world is full of carefully handpicked stories, what people want to present to the world on Instagram or Twitter.

Our world is full of people who have given up, who are selfish because they think there is no love in the world. Selfishness that comes from arrogance, or selfishness that comes from depression or desperation, is still selfishness.

What can save us from this self-involvement?

Love. Self-giving love. Godly love.

One more thing — take these verses home as a meditation and try replacing the word Love with the word Jesus. Jesus bears all things, hopes all things, endures all things. And then imagine yourself by Jesus' side, giving and receiving love. Giving and receiving this deep love that truly cares for others.

Love can save us. May love save us. Amen.

Pumpkin Spice
John 18:33-37

Christ the King Sunday 2018

On a hot day early one September, I went to a local grocery store that has a coffee shop in the store.

Remember, summer technically goes until September 20 or 21. Here in North Carolina, we have hot weather right up until the end of summer. But on this one hot day, a day barely into September, a customer at the coffee shop was loudly requesting a pumpkin spice latte. The customer's friend said, isn't it a little hot outside for a pumpkin latte? To which the customer responded, it's September, isn't it?

This whole pumpkin spice craze began earlier this century, when a certain coffee shop began offering coffee flavored with the same spices one might find in pumpkin pie: nutmeg, clove, and cinnamon. The drink was topped with whipped cream, the same way you might squirt whipped cream from a can on your Thanksgiving pie. In the early version of the beverage, there was no actual pumpkin in the coffee — but I think they have added a bit of pumpkin puree to the mix.

Turns out we have been using the combination of nutmeg, clove and cinnamon for a long time — why? Because it tastes good. Once people discovered that these aromatic spices went will with pumpkin, and apple, and cider, and baked goods... we had autumn all wrapped up. Those aromas have come to signify for us the season of autumn, time with family and friends, and a warm cozy feeling.

So this is the cozy time of year. Time to break out the cozy flavors and fuzzy fleeze and maybe a chunky scarf.

That customer at the coffee shop early in September? It may have been hot outside, but that person was ready to bring on the coziness, the comfort, the feeling of being wrapped up in a warm blanket.

This season we hit maximum cozy. By the time February comes around, we will be sick of cold weather and ice and the only thing to look forward to is March Madness.

In fact, we have some comforting messages coming up in just a few weeks as we celebrate Advent and Christmas. We will sing about "tidings of comfort and joy." We will light Advent candles, which carry encouraging themes:

> Hope
> Peace
> Joy
> Love

Yet there is more. Jesus is coming to change the world. His birth is a challenge to the rulers and powers of this world. His rule is a challenge to the rulers and powers of this world.

Jesus' message is not comfortable for everyone … his message and his presence were certainly uncomfortable for Pilate.

If anyone craves unlimited power, Jesus will make them uncomfortable.

If anyone places race or nationality or citizenship status over the kingdom of God, Jesus will make them uncomfortable.

In the middle of what our culture views as a cozy season, we are going to hear some Scriptures in church that are most definitely not cozy. We will hear about judgment, justice, the rule of Christ.

We will hear about Jesus' coming in power. About John the Baptist, about prophecy, about Mary singing, the low lifted up and the people in high places brought low.

For some time now, it has been a tradition in Presbyterian and similar churches to spend late November and early December reading about Christ's ultimate purposes — his rule overall. We don't spend the entire time leading up to Christmas reading about the baby Jesus himself… but we read about the plans God is making. We read about the rule into which the baby Jesus will grow.

So when we get to Christmas, and we hear again the message that Christ has come into the world, we have already been reminded of his ultimate purpose.

When I began ministry, I didn't like this tradition. I wanted cozy stuff for worship around holiday time. But the world has changed, and I need more than a warm fuzzy feeling. In today's world, I need a message that Jesus is in charge.

But "cozy" is not Jesus' message. Jesus comes to change the world. To challenge the powerful and lift up the lowly.

In about one month we will have a cozy evening here at church on Christmas Eve, so don't worry. Our Christmas Eve lesson and carols service is wonderful. There's a certain sweetness and nostalgia imagining the baby Jesus and snuggled up in the pew with our friends and church family. Now to be honest, our Christmas Eve service is much more than cozy: it's joyful, grand, uplifting. It's everything: can you tell I love our Christmas Eve service?

The message of Jesus on Christmas Eve, and on Christ the King Sunday, and every day, is a message of change.

During Advent and Christmas, pay attention to the songs we sing and the prayers and the Scriptures. They are a message of God coming into the world to change it forever.

This is a message to carry at any time of year — cold weather, hot weather, coffee weather, iced tea weather, whatever. Christ is King. Christ is coming to change the world.

To conclude, I have an invitation for you. I have laid out various candles that have been used during the year here in the sanctuary. Take a candle from church and light it at home. The light will be cozy, and you can even have a latte while watching the flame flicker. I hope the light will be a reminder of Christ's light: the light that shines in the darkness. The light that cannot be overcome. The light shining the way for a new message and a new path.

See you back here for Advent activities and Christmas activities. Thanks be to God for Christ the King. Amen.

They Remembered His Words
John 20:1-18

Easter Sunday

April 21, 2019

I remember words of wisdom from the days when I was young.

My grandmother would say, "Whatever goes around comes around." Sometimes this meant, people get what they deserve, bad or good. Sometimes it meant, history repeats itself.

A pastor once advised me against worrying too much, against taking things personally. He said, trash belongs in the trash can. Meaning, don't waste energy and time on nitpicky things. Don't sweat the small stuff.

I have another type of memory — muscle memory — from my childhood.

My father taught me how to ride a horse. I haven't been horseback riding in years, but I can still remember the instruction, sit light in the saddle.

My mother and grandmother taught me how to snap beans and crowder peas. I haven't snapped a pea in years, but I imagine I could still do it without looking. Pop, pop, pop.

Once you have learned something ... it comes back to you... If you need it, you got this!

Jesus' disciples spent three years learning his words of wisdom. They spent three years building their spiritual muscle, watching him heal, listening to him pray, helping him hand out food to hungry people ... and then, in a span of a few days, everything they learned seemed lost.

Jesus had been crucified — executed. He died the death assigned to a criminal. But he was innocent.

The male disciples, most likely, were marked men. They were known associates of this man Jesus who had been put to death. So, they hid.

The female disciples went to the grave early in the morning, not because they expected resurrection, but because they were fulfilling tradition to anoint a dead body with herbs.

We are so quick to forget what we have learned. So quick to doubt! So quick to dismiss good news as an idle tale.

I believe we have a spiritual memory, like a muscle memory, for God's presence.

The women were using their muscle memory, doing what women in their society were supposed to do... anoint the dead with aromatic herbs and ointments.

Then more memories came back. They heard the angels… why do you look for the living among the dead? And they were shaken from their spiritual slumber. Then they remembered his words … and it began to come back. He's not dead, he's alive! He is with us! We are not alone!

Each time you hear Jesus words it's like that memory becoming fresh again — oh yeah! I know this! I got this!

Jesus advised his disciples that he would suffer (Luke 9:22). He also told his disciples,

'Blessed are the eyes that see what you see! For I tell you that many prophets and kings desired to see what you see, but did not see it, and to hear what you hear, but did not hear it.' (Luke 10:23-24)

Jesus also said, "So I say to you, Ask, and it will be given to you; search, and you will find; knock, and the door will be opened for you." (Luke 11:9)

He told the disciples the Kingdom of God was among them.

These were his words to remember. These were the words that came back to the disciples on that first Easter Day.

We have a spiritual memory too.

We have seen… and heard… and we remember. We have seen people come together in times of tragedy; we have seen people step up to help. We watched the beautiful big church in Paris, Notre Dame, go up in flames. We have seen destruction in our own community this weekend from storms.

We have seen hospital rooms with our own eyes, and we know what happens in those rooms. Sometimes people get better, sometimes they don't. Hospital rooms have a way of making us anxious. And yet we remember the presence of the Holy Spirit in those same anxious places.

We have prayed and felt the power of prayer. We have been lost in the ashes of sadness, in the rubble of disappointment, and someone has come along to sit with us and comfort us.

I remember a tornado when I was in the eighth grade. We woke up to water coming into the house. The men in my family just showed up to help us repair the roof on our house. I still get nervous when I see that funny looking sky, but I remember that day my uncle and cousin and dad worked together, and I know good things can come from bad circumstances.

We are already seeing resurrection in the world around us. God's Kingdom is already among us — we may be asleep to it, maybe have hidden away out of fear, are too doubtful to look around.

This Easter, let us be shaken from our slumber. Let us wake up and tune up that muscle memory.

Why should we continue to hide, in fear and disappointment? Why would we continue to hang around the tomb? It's empty!

Remember his words.

I'll leave you with some words Jesus spoke to seventy helpers whom he sent out:

After this the Lord appointed seventy others and sent them on ahead of him in pairs to every town and place where he himself intended to go. He said to them, "The harvest is plentiful, but the laborers are few; therefore ask the Lord of the harvest to send out laborers into his harvest. Whenever you enter a town and its people welcome you, eat what is set before you; cure the sick who are there, and say to them, "The kingdom of God has come near to you." (Luke 10:1-2, 8-9)

Remember his words. You've got this! The kingdom of God is near. Christ is risen! Alleluia!

www.ingramcontent.com/pod-product-compliance
Lightning Source LLC
Chambersburg PA
CBHW052159110526
44591CB00012B/2011